3

# New Commonwealth Immigrants

Nance Lui Fyson (words)
and Sally Greenhill (photos)

Series adviser: Richard Whitburn
(Social Studies Adviser,
Inner London Education Authority)

## Contents



## Introduction

Only about 2 per cent of the UK population are New Commonwealth immigrants (from all the Commonwealth countries *except* Australia, Canada, and New Zealand). About another 1.2 per cent of the population were born in Britain of New Commonwealth immigrant parents. Where you live in Britain has much to do with how likely you are to know immigrants first hand. New Commonwealth immigrants are a larger part of the population in some areas (e.g. 6.4 per cent of Greater London – but only 0.6 per cent of Scotland).

Is Britain what these immigrants expected? What problems do they and their children face? What efforts are being made to try and sort out these problems?

In the following pages, five people talk about their lives and what it's like to be a black immigrant in Britain. . . .

Macmillan
Education

# Linette Simms

school bus driver

“ . . . To be honest, I'm from a poor family. I always promised that I'd like to help them, also myself. Work was very hard to find in Jamaica.[1] So the only way I could think out was to leave my country and travel out.

I came here because I thought it would be better than my homeland. If things were good there I wouldn't have come here in the first place.[2]

I came here in 1953 on my own. I can remember saying to my mother and a sister, "I want to go to England." They said, "Oh don't be silly. How can you go to England?" I said, "I think I can." They said, "How can you? You haven't got any relatives there, neither any friends." But I said, "I've seen somebody's passport and on the back of it, it says Her Majesty's Government do promise to take care of the bearer in demand." It was my friend's passport. I said, "Oh, if that's a promise, that's a promise! So I'm going to England." Friends and relatives managed to accumulate my fare and I turned to England.

1  More than half of immigrants from the West Indies came from Jamaica. During the Second World War some 7000 West Indians served in the Royal Air Force. Their reports of Britain when they went home encouraged immigrants to come. Most West Indians came to Britain in the years 1950–60.

2  Unemployment and underemployment in much of Asia, Africa, and Latin America is much higher than in Britain. This is why many immigrants have come here — to find jobs. In the mid-1970s, unemployment in Jamaica was about 30 per cent.

When I came here I remember it was a winter night and I landed at Plymouth. I didn't have any address to go to. I didn't have any friends, no one to meet me, and it was night when the boat landed there. I didn't know where to turn. But I remember going to a policeman and saying to him, "Good evening. Can you help me? I arrived in this country and I haven't got anywhere to go." He said, "I beg your pardon." I said, "I haven't got anyone to meet me. I haven't got anywhere to go." He said, "Why you come here then?" I said, "To seek employment." There was another passenger on the same ship who heard me talking to the police, a West Indian lady. And she said to me, "Oh, I heard you talking on the ship that you haven't got anyone to meet you. But I didn't think you were serious. You can come with me. My uncle has got a room provided for me." Just like that. This officer said to her, "Are you sure?" She

said, "Yes, she can come with me." And I went home with her and we shared this room together.

Her relatives got both of us a job the following morning, straight away. My first job was in a tea shop in Piccadilly. My wages was £3 12s 6d per week.[3] Out of that I paid my fares to work, my rent, and look after myself, save. Two or three years after I send for my father.

In Jamaica my father is what you call a cultivator. He work for himself and he will do odd jobs for people to earn some money while he's waiting on his crop to come in. My father never have a cow, never have a horse – but he always have a donkey and pigs and chickens and all that. He have his own house and his own land so he was a bit fortunate there. But I am from a big family. My parents had thirteen of us, eleven of us alive. Money was very scarce because there was no jobs. I just decided to do it my way to help my parents, also myself. Like I said, the second day I landed here I got a job. And I worked from then until now.

3 In late 1953, the average weekly wage for women aged 18 and over was just over £5. The average weekly wage for all workers was just over £8.

I'm married and have six children, four girls and two boys. My first child is 21 years old. They range down to age 8. Three is at school, three out of school. I work in between pregnancies.

I've done steam pressing in a clothing factory and I've done laundry. I was a machinist a few years. I've done driving a lot. I am driving for nineteen years now in this country. I learned to drive here. Now I am driving a 31-seater school bus.[4] I go around picking up children to take them to school. I go on and take other children to swimming, museums, games and all that. I must finish by 3 p.m. so I can take the first set of children back to their houses in the evening. I start at 7.30 a.m. in the morning and finish at 5 p.m. five days a week.

I would criticise this society where young people are concerned. There ain't enough discipline and I blame it down to society. Young people could be better in their behaviour. Teachers should be able to discipline children more. There's not enough discipline at all, not enough manners in school.[5] I think the children I drive are fascinated really and surprised to see a woman as their school bus driver.[6] Coming off and on the bus they don't look where they're stepping. They're looking straight at me. Some of them can't believe their eyes and they shout, "It's a woman! It's a lady!"

With children there is no problem with different races up to the age of 16. As soon as the white children start the age of courtship they start to keep themselves away. I remember a certain English girl on my street. She used to come to my home and play and eat and drink all like one family. Then she started to go out with boyfriends till even she got married. We were surprised to know she didn't even invite us to her

4  Linette Simms is the first woman to drive a school bus for ILEA (the Inner London Education Authority). The Sex Discrimination Act of 1975 has encouraged more women to try for jobs which have in the past been done by men only. In what jobs is it still legal to say that only men (or only women) are wanted?

5  Do you agree?

6  There were 350 men and Linette driving school buses for ILEA in early 1977.

wedding. We were like one family all through the years. Again, there is another white girl on the same street. She play with my children. She got married and they came down and invite us to their wedding. It all depends on the person's mind, not what other people do.

I told my children, ''Marry who you like – black, white, pink, green, red, who you like.'' It doesn't matter to me. Everybody are the same, irrespective to colour. If only people could accept people as they are, it would be a better world. In time it might happen, but I think it might take a long time.

Sometimes in my house you'll have Indians, English, West Indians for the birthday parties and all like that. But I know there is a lot of people that come across discrimination because of their colour.

It is definitely more difficult for young people that are immigrants, with housing, jobs. A boy of 18 could learn to drive, pass his test, buy himself a car – but because of his immigrant background his insurance got to be higher. You have to put on your form your nationality and so on. They really do make it higher.[7]

I would like to see in schools they teach against prejudice. Children should be strongly taught against being prejudiced of people because of their colour.[8]

Some of my own children bluntly told me they do not feel British. They said to me, ''Although we were born here, we are British, we should feel British, but we don't feel British because we are treated so differently.''

I can remember back in the 1950s I happen to go in a hospital

and I could remember people use to come and feel my skin and say, ''Oh, isn't her skin soft.'' They told me they have never seen a coloured person before. Now it's not so because the population has grown so.[9]

This society has been mixed so deep people really have to accept each other's ways. I've been here so long I've acclimatised to the English dishes. But I married a Jamaican and now and again he would like a West Indian dish — rice and peas, curry, green bananas boiled, yam, sweet potato and all like that.[10] Myself and my children would like fish 'n chips, baked beans and chips. My children wouldn't make a proper meal of West Indian food.

I've been back to Jamaica three times. I've brought my father, mother and grandmother here. My father accepted it very well, to stop cultivating the land and come and work here in the post office. My grandmother, who is 95, was in the newspapers. She was one of the oldest passengers to fly from the West Indies to this country.

9  In the early 1950s there were only a few thousand West Indians in Britain. By the mid-1970s there were over 200 000 West Indians in Britain.

10  Have you tasted West Indian dishes? Indian cooking? African cooking?

In Jamaica I never saw any advertising for immigrants to come to Britain. Here I've met people who told me, especially from Barbados, they were recruited by London Transport.[11] They were encouraged to come over.

I heard about discrimination and I know of this but I personally never come across anything like that. I can't say I've ever been turned down for anything because of my colour.

Immigrants come here with very good credentials and qualifications – but because they are immigrants they could not get a job in the field that they would like. Whatever they trained for, they have to take a lower job than what they really want to do.

Only last night I was talking to a certain man from some part of Africa. He's a marine engineer with credentials. He was telling me that when he came here eight or nine years ago and went to get a job in that field they bluntly told him no white man would want to take orders from him.[12] Now he's a school keeper. These insults can be very critical really because some people take it so hard. They just don't want to try any more. It depends a lot on the people.

I remember in the 1960s I applied for an ambulance driving job. I passed all the tests but in the interview, one of the questions was what if I should call at home for a patient and they refused to come with me because of my skin. What would I do? They refuse to let me touch them.[13] I said I would never leave a patient because of that. I would try to show the patient that I am there to help he or she and if they still refuse I would get on the ambulance telephone and talk to someone back at my centre for advice.

It does help if people can get to know people. People should put themselves out to join with people. It will break the barriers. . . .

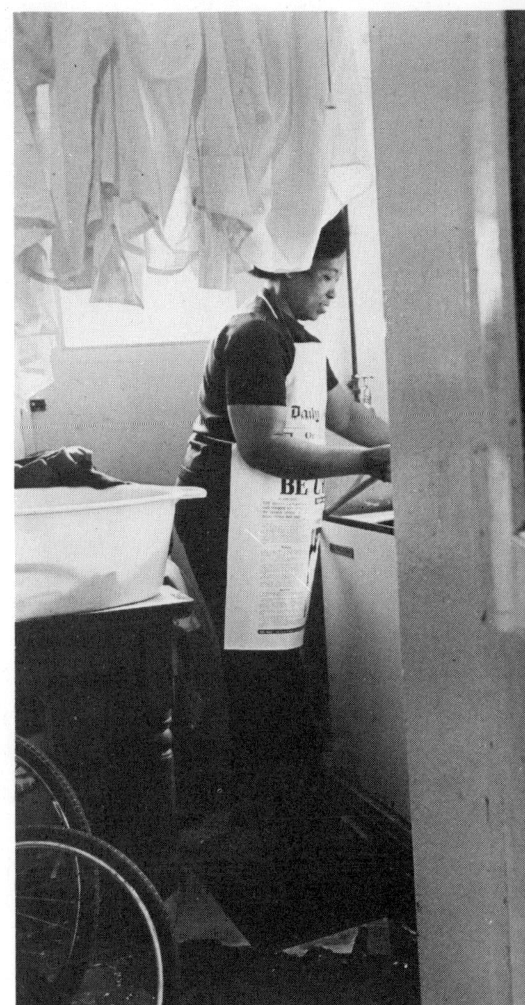

11  London Transport and the British Hotels and Restaurants Association opened recruiting offices in Barbados in the mid-1950s. Britain was then short of unskilled labour, as English workers wanted better jobs.

12  How would you have reacted if you had been turned down from a job for this reason?

13  What would you have said if you had been Linette at that interview? What do you think of her reply?

● Has Linette Simms said anything that:
. . . surprised you?
. . . puzzled you?
. . . shocked you?
. . . worried you?
. . . angered you?

# Ajit Singh Rai

Indian Workers Association,
food store owner

"... I came in the first week of October in 1956, with the idea of returning to my country.

My expectations were that I would be offered a job according to my abilities and qualifications.[1] But what I faced was, first of all, I couldn't get a job. If I could get a job at all it was a night job and the dirtiest job.

I was employed by a rubber factory that was called in those days a "black spot". It was a very dirty firm, making rubber tyres, mats, things like that. I was offered a night shift job at about £8 a week[2]. I was shovelling that rubber into the machines all night. It was a very dirty job. The whole lot of us that came in to this country in the late 1950s had to live with the very crudest type of racial discrimination on the shop floor, by charge-hands, foremen, the whole white staff.

We had to struggle a lot in those days. With my qualifications I could have been offered a clerical job, but that was not a time

1 A university degree.

2 In late 1956 the *average* weekly earnings for manual workers was just over £12.

that we could think of being offered such jobs. The type of jobs we were offered we had to take because we had to live. We were offered only the lowest-paid jobs. We could never argue in those days simply because we were fearing that if we were sacked it would be very hard to find another job. The whole attitude was inflicting injuries to our human dignity, but we had to live with it.

Then, in the early 1960s, people started making up their minds. In the initial stages almost no one knew that he would stay in this country forever. But as people decided to stay, and brought their families, a different set of problems arose – buying houses, finding places for children. . . . My family came one and a half years after I came. One child was born in India – the other three were born here.

There was total racial prejudice in the host community. We were never offered accommodation in host community houses. So what we had to do was buy our own houses. And if they were overcrowded it was because we couldn't find enough places to live.[3] On the outside, normally, people wouldn't show a sign of hating us, but within their minds there was something. We had cases where we were not offered drinks in pubs. We even went to the licensing authority that the pub licence should not be renewed but we did not succeed.[4] All these insults, injuries to our self respect we had to tolerate.

The whole situation started changing as immigration grew. The dependants were joining the fathers. The problems multiplied – problems at the airport, refusing entry to dependants saying, ''You are not the wife of so-and-so'', detaining them at the airports, then schooling, housing. As the number of immigrants increased in this country, the problems increased accordingly.

The role of the Indian Workers Association (IWA) became

3 Cliché slurs on immigrants (like 'They live too many to a house') take little account of the problems immigrants have had in finding houses, etc. What other clichés have you heard about immigrants? Are these based on fact?

4 Laws have since made it illegal to discriminate in pubs, restaurants, etc.

very important. The name was already here, even before the independence of India. But this branch in Southall was built up since 1956 when a few people in this area got together. We enrolled a membership in the first year of not more than 100.[5] I was the first General Secretary for two terms.

The problems in the early days were mostly problems like helping people with new passports and filling out income tax forms. We also wanted some recreation for people because they were totally isolated from the host community. They were lonely people, often working six or seven days a week.

At the beginning of 1957 we started showing Indian films[6] so that people could at least get together at weekends, sit together for two or three hours and forget their difficulties and isolation. We used to rent a cinema at the weekends. With the creation of the IWA and its activities and meetings we had to rent a hall from the local authorities. At one stage the borough education authorities put a ban on the IWA and would not give us a hall for any meeting. The idea came that we must have our own place. That idea materialised in 1965 when we bought the Dominion Cinema.[7] It is now a centre where mostly the Asian community comes for social meetings, receptions, entertainments, films. The separate IWA Welfare Centre is financed from the revenues we make from the cinema. The money we make through the cinema is the only reason the welfare office and services exist.[8] These services we provide to the whole community — whites, blacks, browns. Whoever comes into these offices, if we can help, we help.

In the early 1960s we created the International Friendship Council, Southall. The President was a white. The vice-president was from the IWA. It was a multi-racial group. When the Community Relations Commission[9] came into being, the International Friendship Council was amalgamated into the Ealing CRC. Early in the 1960s the Government was not even willing to think of community councils.

Also, in the early 1960s, the idea came with some host community friends that we should arrange multi-racial pre-

5  In 1976, the Southall-based IWA had some 16 000 members, making it the largest immigrant organisation in the UK. A. S. Rai was the President. (There are other UK branches of the IWA — one in Bradford, and another in Birmingham.)

6  The Indian film industry is the largest in the world. Showing Indian films in Britain offers Indians here some link with their home country. Do you think it is good for immigrant groups to keep their home culture alive — by showing films, dance and music concerts, etc.? Have you ever seen Indian films? Indian dancing?

7  With 1800 seats, this is the biggest centre in the UK showing Indian films.

8  IWA welfare services are many, including language classes, a social centre for old people, support of an Indian youth club, advice on all sorts of legal and social problems.

9  The Community Relations Commission was set up under the Race Relations Act, 1968 to 'encourage the establishment of harmonious community relations'. In 1977 a new organisation called The Commission for Racial Equality replaced the CRC and Race Relations Board.

school playgroups. Children should get together early, before they hear prejudices.[10] We approached the borough council but they said they didn't want to know. They wouldn't give a penny for that project. We had to find the money from our own pockets. We started our project and then we had some help from a trust later on. Later, there were many multi-racial playgroups set up.

We are not only an agency or organisation that is providing services but we are, on behalf of the whole coloured community, trying to put pressure on the Government that they should reverse their bad policies, their bad legislation. Governments have played a part in creating racial discrimination from the top. We are working as a pressure group.[11] Wc are tackling, confronting the whole set of problems facing the whole community.

The media in this country is very powerful. It is not like in our country where many people cannot read and write. The media here has played a very bad role so far as race relations is concerned.[12] The media should have been working to restore the confidence in the minority. Instead, the media has created uncertainty in our community.

The banks were not helpful to our businessmen initially. Once we showed ability, things began to change. Still there are people who don't like us in business. Health inspectors have in many cases played a role prejudicial to ethnic minorities.

The youth problem is also very important. We always argued with the authorities, but they were very slow in doing things for the youth. The youth of our communities became disgruntled not only against the local authorities, but also against their own leadership. As to the gap between parents and children with respect to whether or not we have done something for the future, it is a gap of misunderstanding. Many of the youth do not realise how we have struggled that the whole society should be built up on a multi-racial basis.

In times recently, when things have been very bad for immigrants in this country, there were slogans that the old people should go, that they didn't do anything for the youth. And there was a part of the press that was playing this up and trying to put a wedge between the older members of the immigrant community and the youths. The people who were born here, the "youth", do not have that knowledge of what their fathers have done for themselves in this country. When we came here we were the sufferers of the crudest type of racial discrimination. We could not find good jobs, we could not find day jobs, we were the worst paid. And the people who were handling us were behaving just like we were slaves.

We created things for the new generation. We created homes for them, and then we started fighting for the future. We have been discussing with the education authorities, the Home Office, the council. Our new generation would not stand all

10 Do you think multi-racial playgroups for pre-school children are a good idea?

11 The IWA has campaigned for political candidates, supported overseas freedom fighters, led protests against the bussing of school children, protested against anti-immigrant television programmes, organised demonstrations against laws they see as harmful to immigrants.

12 What examples can you find of newspapers, television, etc., playing a helpful role in encouraging good race relations? What examples can you find of the media not being helpful?

the insults, all the deprivations, all the unfairness which we had to live with in the past.

Coloured community youths must be given equal status. If that status is not given to them there will be conflict, tension, racial violence. This is what we have been trying to make the Government and other sections of the society see. They must see that the time has now come, or rather, that they are already late, to concede to the fact that the children born here, brought up here, are normal English citizens of this country. They must be treated on equal terms for the jobs,[13] for the promotions, for everything – for participating in the political stream of life, or in the trade union movement.[14] They should feel they are belonging to a society where they have got respect and confidence.

Where we were born, we had an entirely different social structure, totally a different civilisation, a different political background and totally a different religious background. Our children who were born here live two lives, one at their homes and another in the outside world. They have not totally left their own background, and they have not totally adopted the new one. There must be compromise. The parents should concede to the fact that they are not living back in their own country. The children who are born here should give some concession to their parents who were born in a different atmosphere. These social problems are creating very deep tensions within the families. It will take some time before it all settles down.

13  Department of Employment figures show that in times of recession coloured workers are much more likely to be unemployed than white workers. From November 1973 to May 1975 overall unemployment rose 65 per cent in Britain — but the number of coloured people unemployed rose 156 per cent. The IWA Welfare Centre runs English classes for unemployed Asian youths to help their chances at gaining a job. They also advise young people on job training.

14  The IWA is concerned that white-dominated British trade unions should protect the interests of immigrant workers. The IWA is encouraging immigrants to work within the existing unions.

Any section of the community, whether new or old, if they don't know where they belong, if they don't know their history, if they have got no roots, would be a lost section. It would not be a healthy section of the community. If they know they belong to some place, if they know they belong to some culture and civilisation, politics, religion, way of life, then they know they have got roots. That would definitely help. It would reflect on their minds. They have got the background of thousands of years behind them.[15] If they are cut off from their old way of life and they are not fitted into the new one, that is a lost section. It could be a most dangerous, irresponsible section of the community.

We are still facing racial discrimination now in almost all forms of life. The difference now is that the ethnic minorities have started asserting themselves. There is increasing realisation on the part of the Goverment, the TUC, the Labour party, the Tory party, the Queen. She gave a reception the other day at Buckingham Palace for the leaders of the minorities. This is a very big change. This shows that they have accepted us. By their gesture they are demonstrating to their own people to accept us, give us the respect we need.[16]

The new Race Relations Act (1976)[17] is much better, much stronger. . . .

15  The IWA also suggests to education authorities that more Asian culture should be included in schools here (Asian games, languages, etc.). This would give young people of Asian background more under-standing of their roots and also enrich other children in schools.

16  Does it have an effect on public opinion when politicians and other leaders speak out on the subject of immigrants? Do you think UK leaders have done enough to encourage good race relations?

17  The Race Relations Act, 1976 is much bolder and more far-reaching than earlier Race Relations Acts of 1965 and 1968. The 1976 Act tackles patterns of discrimination in society. Is passing laws to stop discrimination a good way of changing the way people feel about immigrants?

● Has A. S. Rai said anything that:
. . . surprised you?
. . . puzzled you?
. . . shocked you?
. . . worried you?
. . . angered you?

# Felix Cobbson

teacher of African art,
music and dance



. . . I decided that if I had talent in art it would be nice to have some training. But there wasn't any art college in Ghana [there is now]. So I applied to St Martin's College of Art in London and was accepted.[1]

No, Britain wasn't at all what I expected it to be! At home when somebody talks about Britain the impression of the place is maybe the whole street is lined with gold, you wouldn't find a piece of litter anywhere, the whole place is clean. Oh yes, this is the impression because one has heard of Buckingham Palace! The Houses of Parliament! Big Ben! Westminster Abbey! You think that it is another world completely.[2]

But when I arrived at Liverpool I said, "What! Is this England?" I saw a lot of white people carrying things up and down, pushing trolleys. I didn't think English people did those jobs! What knocked me out completely was a white shoe shiner asking if I would like my shoes polished! I was

1  Felix came to England at the age of 18. After leaving school, he at first tried dentistry and teaching before deciding to train in art.

2  What ideas do you have about places to which you've never been: say New York or Calcutta? Do you think you would be very surprised if you went and saw the places as they really are?

really surprised when I landed in England. It was just the opposite of what I expected, seeing white people doing manual jobs, some of them wearing tatty clothes, and even people by the roadside, tramps. I thought everybody would be in a very smart suit, bowler hat, umbrella, every single person![3]
When I arrived I lived with my uncle's friend who then worked for the Ghana embassy.[4] Then after a few months I

3 People coming from ex-colonies were used to seeing the colonial civil servants from Britain who worked in places like Ghana. For many, this was their idea of what every English person was like.

4 The chain pattern of immigration is very common. Immigrants already here help

left his place and I rented a room. As far as art school was concerned, I didn't meet any form of prejudice at all. In fact, it was just the other way around. Most of the students invited me to see their parents and during Christmas I was invited to stay with some families. After a year one of the students said he would like me to come and live in his grandfather's house. Since I came to Britain I honestly haven't met any form of prejudice, not at all, no.[5]
After I trained as a graphic artist, I got a job in Harlow New Town teaching art. One day we were doing object drawing. I took some drums to school and had the drums arranged for the children to draw. When the bell rang for break they all rushed to the drums and started playing them. I said, "Do you like the drums?" They all said, "Yeah! could we play them?" I said, "Yes, of course." Then they asked if they could come back again during the lunch hour and I said, "Look, if you're that keen I'll teach you how to play African music." They all said, "Yes!" The enthusiasm! I was surprised. I thought that maybe

newcomers by offering a place to stay until housing is found.

5 Do you think most New Commonwealth immigrants experience some form of prejudice?

because the drums were more or less foreign to them that their reaction would be no, we've not going to touch them.[6] They came during the lunch hour and we began having lessons. We participated in the school fete with African drumming and dancing. The press came and there was a big thing "Black Jazz Comes to Harlow New Town". That's how my teaching African music and dance all started.

Then just two years ago there was a new post for Director of Creative Activities at Stewart's School where I am now. And so African drumming and dance became part of the school's curriculum.

Teaching the children African music was tough at the beginning because they had never heard real African music.[7] They found a cross-rhythm a bit off-putting. You teach one boy to start a rhythm and then you teach a second boy to follow the rhythm playing quite different patterns. The second person upsets the first person. But after they got used to it, they began to do it well. I think they do it very well indeed. They enjoy it and we have more and more children coming in every day wanting to take part.

Now the young people know that African music is not just taking the drums and banging. No, not at all. We in Africa drum for a purpose. We have traditional music. We have social music. Traditional music may be for the harvest, for death, for birth, war, victory. We have music for everything. I explain to the pupils that this kind of drumming is a war dance and it's only played on certain occasions. Then we have *agbadza* which is played during funerals. Then we have heal-

6  What would your reaction have been? Would you have wanted to play the drums?

7  Have you? Have you heard Indian music? Chinese music? West Indian music? Do you like what you have heard?

ing music like *tigari* and *nana*. Then there is social music which is played for a wedding or when people collect together to have fun. Social music can be played at any time of the year but traditional music is played at certain times of the year only, and only on special occasions. The pupils know all this and they know the historical background of the drums. Drumming and dancing is part of the everyday life of the African. It means a lot to us.

It depressed me a lot to hear what my pupils knew of Africa. In my country houses are almost all detached with plenty of land, trees, space. We paint our houses nice colours – yellows and reds and greens. But the kids here don't know anything of this modern housing at all. Their impression is only the grass roofs and mud huts. I don't think schools here teach enough about Africa. Westerners show a lot on television and in books of the festivals where we dress up and wear masks because it is fascinating. But what about the ordinary African life? Not enough of that is shown. No wonder the children have such strange ideas about Africa.[8]

I don't think African music and art is really understood by the Western world.[9] We need more people to educate people in this part of the world about African culture. Since I have started this African music and dance in Harlow we have performed many places. The reception has been fantastic.

I think Britain has got a lot to learn from Africa, because of our community life. We live together, do things together. People matter to us. Old people are part of the family. They live with us. They are our encyclopedia. There are a lot of customs and

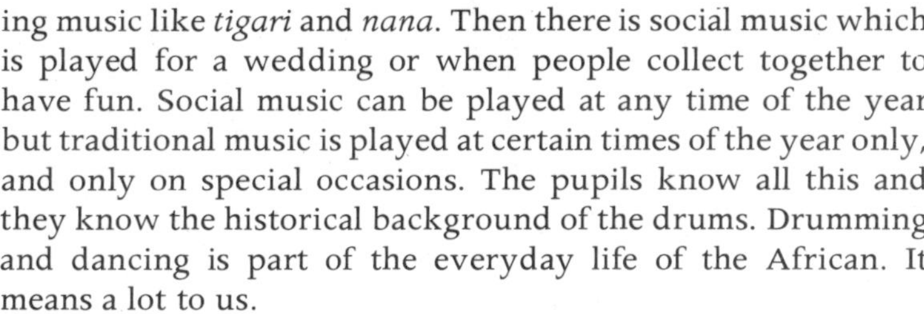

8 What do you think of when the word 'Africa' is mentioned? Factories? Supermarkets? Telephones? These are all there. Where have your ideas of what Africa is like come from? Do you have any idea about ordinary, everyday life in Africa (or Jamaica, or India)?

9 Do you think this is so? Have you seen African sculpture, fabric printing, masks, or pottery? What do you think of the African arts and crafts you have seen? Do you understand what they are about?

traditions which we haven't got down on paper. We learn these from our elders. We go to them for advice, for direction. But in this part of the world only a husband, wife and kids form the family. Old people are pushed to the side. Old people here may be lonely with no one to talk to for weeks or months. That would never, never happen in Africa. It is in things like this that I think Britain has got a lot to learn from Africa.[10] Discipline in Britain is very bad. In Africa we teach our children to be humble and to respect their elders, to accept direction from those that came before them. We say to young people, "You will get what you need, not what you want". Every single person in the society is concerned with the upbringing of children. When a child is doing something wrong any elderly person will stop and say, "You will not do this". Here people just walk past, nobody says anything. And the children think if you are not their mum or dad you have no right to tell them anything. Until I came to this country I never heard the word vandal. In Africa you don't have youngsters going about smashing things up. There must be some form of punishment for the child to know he can't get away with things.[11]

There are thousands of children at home who don't have the advantages we have here for education.[12] The children here don't appreciate what they have got.

I think immigration to England must be controlled. Because of the false impression which most people in Africa and other places have of England, everybody wants to come here.[13] Now in almost all the African countries we've got medical schools, engineering schools. People can have this sort of tuition at home. They must appreciate that what we do in Africa is as good as what is done in the Western world. People in Africa want English goods, English shirts, English marmalade. It might be because of colonial rule that they think everything made in England must be the best. This prejudice must be removed. Until we educate our children in Africa to understand that England is not all gold then most of them would still like to come to this part of the world. Immigration must be controlled – for their own interests.

There should be lots and lots of black and white cultural activities in Britain. This is the beginning of bringing black and white together. We must have cultural exchange. Not many people in Britain know the real African, the background of the African. Prejudice against blacks may be fear of the unknown.[14] We've got to start with the children, the teenagers. The schools should start. I've heard some children saying things like, "The black people come here and take all our jobs" or "The black people come here to take our houses". This just isn't true.[15] Somebody must tell them.

I've been back to Africa about four times and I'll be going back again at Christmas. It worries me a lot when I see that some people there still cling to the idea that things from the West

10  Do you agree that Britain is not as 'caring' a society as it could be (of old people, the handicapped, etc.)? What do you see around you of the way people treat other people that you think needs to be changed? Does the fact that Britain is a more industrial, more urban place than most of Africa account for some of the differences in family and community life? (Britain is 76 per cent, Ghana only 29 per cent, urban. Also, Britain has a much higher proportion of old people.)

11  Do you agree? Is there too little discipline in British schools?

12  In Africa, only 48 per cent of primary-age children are at school. Only 25 per cent of secondary-age children are at school. Only 1.5 per cent of older young people are in higher education. Most parents want schooling for their children – but in poorer countries there are simply not enough schools, books, or teachers. More children go to school in Asia and Latin America – but still a much smaller percentage than in Britain. A much larger part of the population in Ghana (47 per cent) is under 15, compared to only 24 per cent in Britain. This makes it all the harder for countries like Ghana to provide schooling for everyone.

13  While many overseas impressions of Britain are false – the feeling that Britain is a richer place *in money terms* is true. GNP (Gross National Product) per person in Britain is nearly ten times that of Ghana (and more than twice that of Jamaica, and nearly twenty times that of India). Average life expectancy in Britain is about 72 – compared to 44 in Ghana. In Ghana, 156 out of every 1000 babies born do not live to their first birthday. (In Britain, only 16 of every 1000 babies do not live to their first birthday.) Just as people from poorer countries (like Ghana) are attracted to a richer country like Britain, so nearly half of all the people *leaving Britain* emigrate to Australia, New Zealand, and Canada (all with a higher GNP per person than Britain).

14  Do you think people would be less prejudiced against immigrants if they knew more of them personally?

15  New Commonwealth immigrants to Britain were only 28 per cent of all immigrants to the UK in 1975. (In fact, more people *left* Britain in 1975 than came in.) Of the 3.2 per cent of the UK population that is of New Commonwealth origin, 40 per cent were in fact born in the UK. New Commonwealth

are better.[16] When I go back, as I did in 1971, and see my people drumming and dancing, the wood carvers, the fabric printers, all the children participating in the villages, mum and dad, brothers and sisters, I just stood back and said, "By gum, we've got something. This is fantastic!" I stood there and said, "Look, I'm nobody. This is it. This is what life is all about. And look at me. I've gone to England. I've been to an art college. Here are these people. They've never been to an art college and look at the work they do!" I'd like to see more immigrants going back and telling people in their own countries what England is really like. It would help a lot. If you can do it at home, stay. There's no need to come to England at all.[17]

I think one of the worst damages of colonial rule was that so much of our art was taken and brought to England and other places. Our wood carvings, our gold jewellery. We haven't got museums filled with the evidence of what our ancestors did, as you have here. And when people here to to a museum and see African art they never think how it got here. We need to have these things at home to educate our children. Everything that Britain took from other countries during colonial days they should return to them. . . .[18]

immigrants generally make *smaller* demands on the social services because a higher proportion are of working age. Asians and West Indians rely far less on council housing than the native British population. (Three-quarters of all Asians in Britain own their own houses.)

16 Is wanting to come to Britain part of this feeling, left over from colonial days, that Western things (shirts, soft drinks, etc.) are better than native, traditional African products? Can you see why it worries Felix Cobbson (and others) to see some Africans losing pride in all that is rich and valuable in their own culture?

17 A reason why many New Commonwealth immigrants want to come to Britain is the shortage of jobs in their own countries. Unemployment is as high as 30 per cent of the work force in some places. Creating more job opportunities in poorer countries depends on these countries having a better deal in world trade. Richer countries, like Britain, have long dominated world trade and organised it to their own advantage.

18 What do you think of this? How important is it for children to see the art produced by generations before them? Does it help to give children a pride in their own country and own culture?

● Has Felix Cobbson said anything that:
. . . surprised you?
. . . puzzled you?
. . . shocked you?
. . . worried you?
. . . angered you?

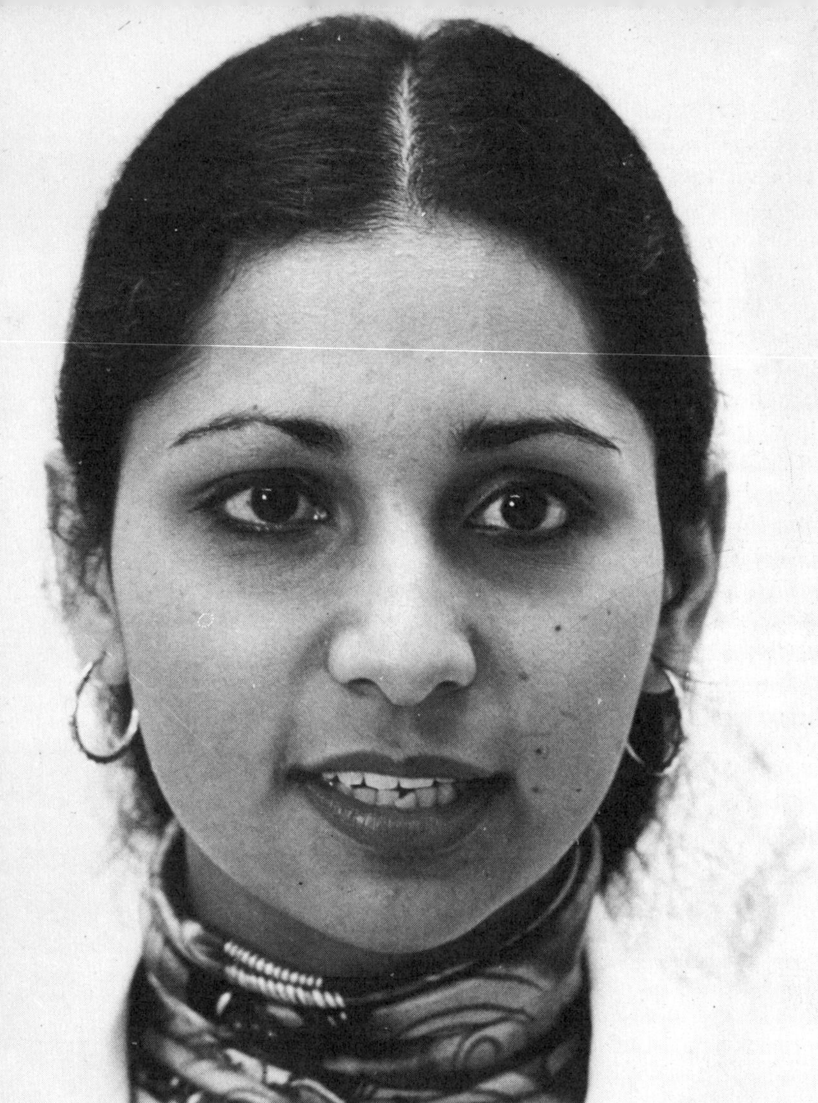

# Bhupinder Kaur Sandhu

doctor

" . . . When I first came to this country[1] I came with the rest of my family. I don't really remember very clearly what I expected Britain to be like, but I do remember not being able to tell the difference between white people.[2] I used to get all the characters on television mixed up. In India I had only seen about three or four white people.

My family left India[3] partly because my mother didn't really get on very well with her mother-in-law. In India, the joint or extended family[4] consists of the oldest male who is the head and then all the sons. The daughters are married off and they go and join their prospective families. For a daughter-in-law to come into a family is a very stressful situation. She really has to be accepted in order for the whole thing to work. In India you hear lots of songs, myths and stories about the conflict when the mother-in-law and daughter-in-law do not get on. While the joint family provides security, it puts a big strain on

1 Bhupinder came at the age of 11. Do you think it is easier to resettle if you come to a new country as a very young person?

2 Does this surprise you? Have you heard anything like this before?

3 Bhupinder's family came from the Punjab. Most Indian immigrants in Britain are from the Punjab (north of Delhi) or from Gujarat (north of Bombay). Find these areas on a map of India.

4 The traditional Indian family is much larger and more complex than the English family unit. The oldest male is the authority, who arranges marriages, etc. Old people are looked after by the young. What advantages and disadvantages do you see for several generations living together?

your individuality. You can't just go and do what you want. You can only do what is accepted within the family system. While it would not have been the accepted thing for my parents to have set up a separate house near my father's family, it was quite acceptable to go away to another city. My father[5] didn't really want to come, but he had been to England earlier[6] on so he thought perhaps we'd make another go of it. Also, he thought he could give his three children a better education. As far as prejudice goes, when I first came I came into a rather closely-knit Indian community. There was another Indian girl in my year at school and I stuck quite close to her. I think I was more aware of being Indian then and when people reacted to me differently I didn't mind so much. I think my father has



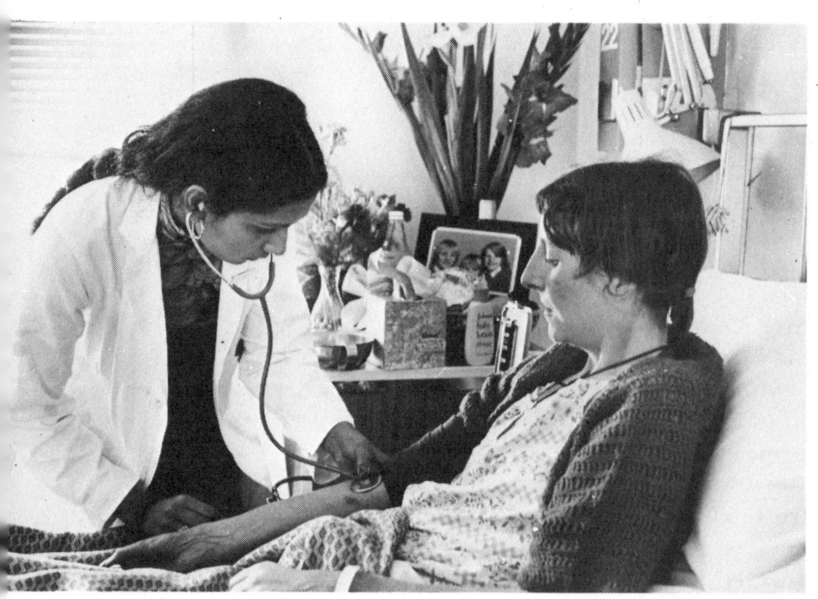

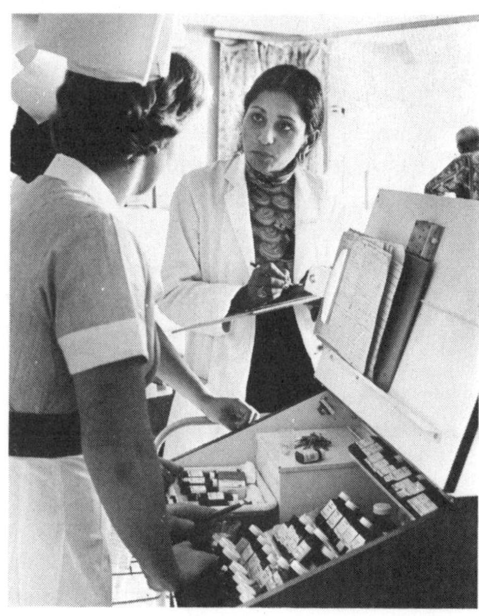

met far more prejudice than I have. When a person is trained in India and comes to do a job here, there is always doubt about whether or not they are competent.[7] This is where I think perhaps my experience is different from another doctor who would have qualified in India, because once I say I have qualified at University College Hospital in London there is a link between me and the other people.

Immigrant doctors are somewhat discriminated against in the Health Service.[8] You hardly see any immigrant doctors in teaching hospitals. The few that are there are usually on scholarships or have come for a year to study a particular topic and then go back. You don't really get the immigrant doctors getting reasonable posts in teaching hospitals. Immigrant doctors tend to work in hospitals that are the least equipped and also within departments that aren't popular with English doctors.[9] Some consultants are so prejudiced that they will look at a list of applicants for a job and anybody who has a foreign name just doesn't get interview. Anybody who is white gets preference as compared with an Indian doctor unless the person is known.

I think the initial reaction of patients is "Perhaps he or she isn't as good as a white doctor".[10] I think the relationship changes once you actually get to know the person. I have come across patients who initially have said, "Oh, another Indian doctor!" In a way one hopes to change their views and make them realise that you are a person concerned about their health and they are a person to you, regardless of the colour difference between you.

When I was in the sixth form I was very much set on going to a country which needed doctors far more than Britain. I would still like to do that. I think India[11] would probably be most suitable because I can speak Hindi and Punjabi. I could then communicate with the patients and I would know the cultural set-up. You can be a better doctor if you can understand the cultural background of your patients.[12] However, at the moment I don't really feel ready to embark on this and am reasonably happy working in this country. I feel I would need to learn a lot more to be able to cope in a hospital without the facilities which are provided here.

I think both India and England have their good points and bad points. Now, having lived here more than half my life I feel quite at home in the set-up in which I find myself. Although I wonder where I am when an old lady patient says to me, "How do you like my country?" I wonder whether she's lived most of her life here and compared to that my twelve or thirteen years are nothing. But yet to me it is most of my impressionable life and I wonder whether to say, "Yes, I like your country" or "Well, it's my country too".

I think something lacking in this society is respect for the older people.[13] They seem to be an unwanted product that is left over. In India there is a respectability about being old and everybody looks up to the old people and listens to their advice. But on other things, such as the role of women in traditional Indian society, I see the need for change. In India in the old days a woman was just kept at home, looked after by the man, and she provided the children and looked after them. She had very little to say about what was actually happening to her.[14] She grew up within a family, her marriage was arranged and she had to marry whomever was chosen for her by the parents.

An arranged marriage requires thinking in a special way. What happens is that the girl and the boy have never had any sort of experiences with anyone else and, as soon as the girl is told that she is going to be married to this person, she falls in love with the idea of him as a perfect mate. That's the only sort of set-up in which it can work. As they meet and get to know each other they gradually fall in love with each other. Then they have the children to bring them together. The whole thing depends on respect for each other and learning

10  Do you think this is so?

11  While Britain has one doctor for every 800 people, India has one doctor for every 5000. Richer countries like Britain are drawing to them doctors badly needed in their home countries. The training foreign doctors receive here is often not right for the kinds of health problems most important in their own countries. Also, immigrant doctors are learning to rely on expensive equipment, drugs, etc. which are not as readily available in their own countries.

12  Do you think this is important? Some overseas doctors have difficulty in understanding British slang. A *Manual of English for the Overseas Doctor* lists twenty-four ways to say 'pregnant'. It lists slang terms for parts of the body — and explains which terms are polite and which are rude.

13  Is Bhupinder right in her criticism of how old people are treated in Britain? Are they respected?

14  The role of women is undergoing some change in many places. What advantages and disadvantages are there for women living in a society where they have little obligation to arrange life for themselves? What problems are there for women having more freedom?

15  Do you think people can learn to love each other? Do you think this kind of marriage can work? While the reformed 1955 law in India allows divorce, the rate is very low. How important are expectations to marriage?

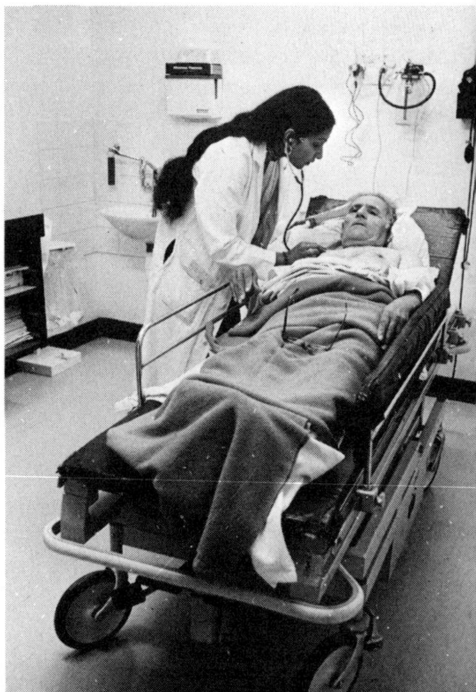

to care for each other.[15] Traditional Indian parents in this country regard English society as very promiscuous. They say, "Oh well, look at them. The marriages don't last a day. Everybody goes round sleeping with everybody."[16] They just don't want that sort of life for their children.

An Indian girl here is supposed to stay at home and have an arranged marriage and then be a mother and a good housewife. The girl goes to school and she comes across other girls, English girls, who are going out in the evenings, who have boyfriends and who talk about them and the sort of person they are going to marry. With a rigid Indian family set-up the Indian girl is not really allowed to experiment and this can lead to a lot of stress and difficulties in the relationship between the parents and the girl.[17] Her mother has probably accepted an arranged marriage without any questioning whatsoever, and it is very hard for her to realise why her daughter is resisting.[18]

I think that the immigrant parents living here do change over the years and the children have an accelerating effect on this change, because they are bringing in new ideas into the family. I have seen my parents' views change over the years. I think the problems arise when the parents are very rigid and don't change at all, and the children are just fighting against a wall. Personally I like to see an integrated society rather than the Indians living in a little corner on their own[19] and West Indians in another little corner, etc. I would like to see a lot more integration and yet see the different communities retaining some of their traditions. One of the reasons why the close-knit Indian community came to be is that it provides protection from the hostility of the English population. For Indian women who speak English poorly or not at all,[20] the efforts of friendly English neighbours could mean a lot.

16 Do you think people should live with different people before they marry? Are they more likely to find a 'right' partner this way?

17 What sort of difficulties do young people born here to immigrant parents have in feeling British — and yet not British?

18 Could you accept the idea of an arranged marriage for yourself? What are the advantages and disadvantages of having a partner chosen by parents?

19 Of the major immigrant groups in Britain, Indians have the lowest rate of intermarriage with British.

20 Language is often a problem for immigrants of all races. There are over 100 000 who know little or no English. Asians who have come to the UK in the last twenty years are the largest group in this category. What efforts are being made to teach English to immigrants?

My mother in fact is of a Hindu background but married into
a Sikh family.[21] For me, I don't think this mixed background
provided any difficulties at all. In a way it enriched my
experiences. I know a bit about Hinduism from my mother
and my maternal grandparents and a bit about Sikhism[22] from
my father and his family. I don't really feel that I belong to any
religion at all. Even if I did I don't think it makes a lot of
difference what you call the god if you believe in a god. The
really important aspects of all the religions are very similiar,[23]
like not doing harm to other people and not taking lives and
trying to live an honest life.

As far as British politics are concerned, I think at the present
that immigrants feel very much withdrawn, not quite ready to
participate in ordinary day-to-day politics of the country. The
British community is still very rejecting of anybody else
coming from outside into it and the idea of having an Indian
MP or something would seem alien to most people.[24] The
older Indians have their own organisations like the Indian
Workers Association but they are very reluctant to participate
within the party politics of this country.

As for the police, I think initially I was quite pleased with the
way the police acted, but since then my ideas have changed.
The police force here seem to be pretty prejudiced in their

views. They think that the black kids, especially the West Indians, are more likely to be making trouble.[25] I think the Indian community feels to some extent that if it came to the police protecting the whites or the Indians they would protect the whites.

At the moment immigrants tend to do a lot worse than what they would do if they were part of the native British population. They end up getting the worst jobs usually.[26] Most of them seem to be living in areas where the housing and education facilities are poorer,[27] hence things are weighed against them before they start. On top of that they have the prejudices which the outside world has towards them. Often one hears on the media that immigrants aren't really wanted, that they are parasites and why don't they go home.[28] It's not really the best sort of circumstances for an immigrant kid to grow up in. I see the solution as more integration and for the native population to realise that the immigrant people are also people.[29] They should be accepted as people and not just looked at as a separate entity. I realise that this means the immigrant population perhaps losing their identity to some extent[30] – but this is better than having isolated and bitter ghettoes. . . .

25  Do you think the police are prejudiced against New Commonwealth immigrants? Why might immigrants think this to be so?

26  Most Indians here are employed in unskilled or semi-skilled work in industry or public transport. Few gain white-collar jobs even if they have been teachers or civil servants in India. Seventy-six per cent of Indian wage earners here work in manual jobs, compared to 51.2 per cent of British wage earners. Are laws enough to stop discrimination in job opportunities, housing, etc.?

27  There are two groups of Indian settlements. The oldest are the pre-war port settlements. The settlements since the Second World War are mostly in inland towns and cities. Which British towns and cities have sizeable Indian communities?

28  Do most people in Britain regard immigrants as parasites? Would most British want immigrants to go home? What arguments would you use to persuade people that immigrants make a positive contribution to Britain?

29  What laws are there to encourage better race relations? What efforts has Britain made to understand and help the problems of immigrants?

30  To what extent should immigrant groups become 'like the British'?

● Has Bhupinder Kaur Sandhu said anything that:
. . . surprised you?
. . . puzzled you?
. . . shocked you?
. . . worried you?
. . . angered you?

# Ashton Gibson

Westindian Concern Ltd

“ . . . No, Britain was certainly not what I expected. I suppose like most West Indians we had our own dreams of this country. I don't think that you can be educated, inculcated with the best of British history without feeling a part of it. Therefore in 1952 I came here[1] an Englishman – no two ways about it.

I came here basically to do accountancy, not because I wanted to work as an auditor but because I was genuinely interested in business and it seemed a means of raising to the boardroom of a company. One's expectations were definitely pitched high. You felt if one mastered the skills and the ability one would be able to make it but it didn't take you very long to know that there were no skills that could be acquired that could overcome the prejudices that were very real in those days. Yes, it has been a great disappointment indeed. I think the greatest disappointment has been the apathy. The British have no appreciation of the suffering of immigrants in this country.[2]

1  From Barbados.

2  Do you agree? Do you think New Commonwealth immigrants have been Britain's 'scapegoats' in the 1950s, 60s, and 70s? (Scapegoat comes from an old Hebrew ritual of taking a live goat, putting all the sins and guilt of the people on to it, and then sacrificing the goat. The people then felt better. The term has come to mean blaming someone else for our own difficulties and misfortunes. By putting the blame on to other people we feel better. By looking down on other people we try to make ourselves feel bigger. In Britain the Irish were the scapegoats in the 1930s, the Jews and East Europeans in the 1940s. New Commonwealth immigrants have been easy to recognise as a separate group on to whom 'blame' could be put.)

26

I know a friend who came to this country about the same time as me. He taught in Barbados. He was a damn good teacher but he just couldn't get a job here. He saw a job advertised for Dr Barnardo's. He applied but wasn't even short-listed because he was told the children wouldn't understand. He took it very hard.[3] He ended up taking a job on the buses as a conductor. Today he's an inspector. When we came here in the early days we did apply for jobs with the police, the social services . . . there was no chance.

I am not speaking about immigrant groups generally. I am speaking about West Indians who are suffering deprivation over and above even other groups with colour. The pressures on all immigrants are the same. Some are equipped to cope, others are not.

The West Indian is in a dreamland. He doesn't know where he is, who he is, where he is going. Slavery has really taken away his culture. Slavery was only abolished in the last century. The Asians have not a legacy of slavery. They have been able to bring with them a strong culture and a strong religion and ability to keep together. They have been able to protect their children against the alienation which the West Indian has not been able to do. And the result is that there are more Asians working in government departments and joining in all over the place than you'll see West Indians. You don't see the Asians flooding out the educationally sub-normal schools,[4] crowding out the police courts and borstals.[5] So let's face it, it's not fair to lump the West Indian with other immigrant groups. You have to look at it in West Indian terms.

At Westindian Concern Ltd[6] our main work is an active counselling programme in the community. Our people come from a much more simple society. They need to adjust on their own terms. West Indians are ashamed of their problems. Why?

3 How would you have reacted if you'd been turned down that way?

4 While Asians fully educated in Britain are doing as well in school as the British, those pupils with a West Indian background are not. West Indian young people are in ESN (educationally sub-normal) schools in a much higher proportion. But this does *not* mean that pupils with a West Indian background have overall lower ability. Language problems are one reason why many have fallen behind. Tests have also shown that how people perform is strongly affected by their feeling of relative social position. A person's actual ability may be high — but if he feels himself in a socially low position, he may not do well.

5 Young people, generally, are more likely to get in trouble with the law than older people. A much larger proportion of people of West Indian origin are under age 25 than in the population as a whole (or in other immigrant groups). In 1977 over half of the West Indian community was under the age of 15 — more than twice the figure for the total population.

6 Westindian Concern Ltd was founded in 1975 by Ashton Gibson. Besides advising and helping West Indians, the organisation helps and advises teachers, police, social workers, etc. whose work brings them into contact with West Indians. The staff are all West Indian. Caribbean House is the headquarters and social centre for youth and adults.

Why does an old age pensioner freeze to death instead of drawing the grant to which they are entitled? It's because of the kind of society you've got. The inadequate blame themselves for their disadvantage.[7]

We are addressing ourselves exclusively to the West Indian community. We are trying to stop the authorities from doing things that are damaging our community. We are trying to educate the authorities ourselves.

We are financed totally from the West Indian community itself. Membership fees to Caribbean House contribute, and we have weekend parties for which we charge extra on refreshments. These and other activities give us a small income.

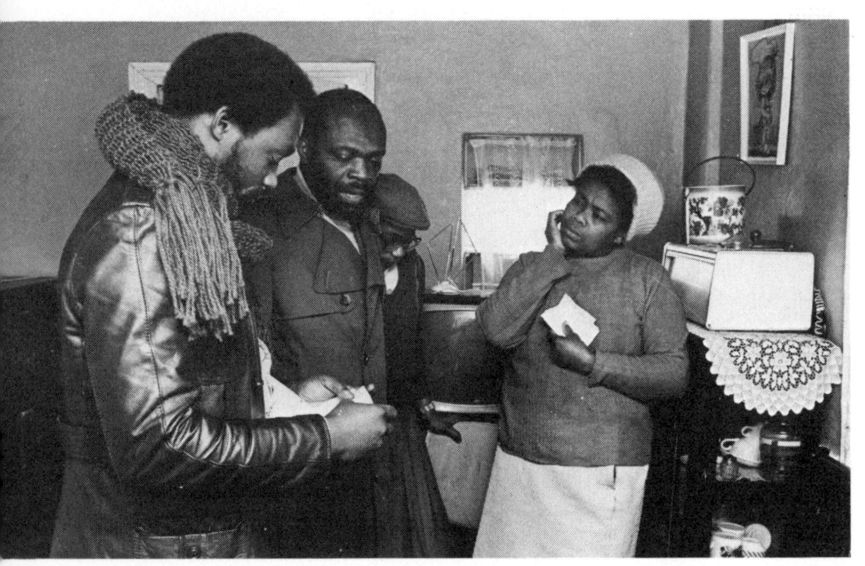

Before Westindian Concern Ltd, I founded an organisation in 1971 called Melting Pot – the largest West Indian organisation in the country. Even though I founded it, gave birth to it, I got out because I was unable to change what was happening. It was set up originally just like this, to help the West Indian community as a whole. But a lot of people came from government departments and offered money to help us do things, and we fell for it. An example will show how this can all go wrong. One thing we were doing was housing about 200 homeless children in hostels, with the emphasis on getting them back to their homes. Society makes it very easy for the children of West Indians to reject their parents. They have the same low regard for their parents as the rest of society.[8] The council stepped in and provided luxurious accommodation and pocket money for the homeless, which was making it totally impossible to get them back home. It was only driving them farther away. So we started Westindian Concern Ltd. We are against accepting outside money.[9]

The reason why we cannot be a charity is that we have got to

7 Why do people not claim government benefits to which they are entitled? To what extent is it one's own fault if one is poor? A 1977 survey on how people in all EEC countries felt about poverty showed that a larger proportion of British, more than any other country, think the poor have only themselves to blame. Only about 16 per cent of Britons blame 'injustice in our society' compared with 26 per cent in the EEC as a whole.

8 West Indians are, on the whole, at the bottom of UK society (in wages, type of work, job security, housing, education, political power, etc.). Young people, seeing their parents on a low rung, may think that there is some natural inferiority putting their parents there — instead of realising all the historical and cultural reasons why West Indians have been at a disadvantage. Young people may react by running away from home as a way of denying they are part of the minority group. Westindian Concern Ltd is trying to improve the image and real social and economic position of the West Indian in Britain.

9 What are the advantages and disadvantages of an organisation working for social change receiving funds from the Government and other outside sources?

fight some of our problems on a political level and in the courts. These are not in the terms of reference of a charity.[10] Even the institutions that you have got set up for the disadvantaged to help themselves aren't even up to the situation. In the end there is always that measure of compromise. People have got to have independence.

Here at Caribbean House there is sharing, talking, so that they discover that things are not what they should be. Many of the things they take for granted should not be taken for granted at all. This is a centre where they come in their own setting, their own surroundings and continue the process of awareness. This is a getting together.

Because of our alienation we have not been able to protect our children against alienation. We only notice the alienation of the children, but the parents who have been here fifteen or twenty years do not know how much they are alienated as well. British society has a very friendly attitude towards our children and a very unfriendly one towards the parents.[11] The situation is worse, far worse now than when I came here. Worse because although there have been some obvious improvements, there haven't been enough to withstand the shock of everything that has gone before.

If you think things have improved because you have made more positions and set up more departments so you can point to people that are doing something – it's for yourself, not for us.

The big problem for us is that British society is faced two ways. You have welfare services intended to benefit the disadvantaged. Yet when the disadvantaged claim, there's a double attitude towards them. They're made to feel wrong for claiming.[12]

10 How many charities are there in the UK? What is the Charities Commission? Are charities allowed to be involved with political activity?

11 A 1976 sample survey of British adults did indeed find a difference in feelings towards coloured immigrants and towards their children. Only 16 per cent were sympathetic towards coloured immigrants — but 45 per cent were sympathetic towards coloured people *born in Britain*. Twenty-five per cent were hostile towards coloured immigrants, but 8 per cent were hostile towards coloured people *born in Britain*.

12 Do you think this is so?

All the professional organisations imbue a sense of helplessness in ordinary people – so you can't help yourself. This is bad.[13] The media is corrupt from right to left, top to bottom. But no more corrupt than other institutions in the country. I went to see a governor of a borstal. He said to me he was very concerned, at the end of his tether because of West Indian boys in his borstal. He had to tell me what he was telling me in confidence. He can't even let the world at large know that he can't cope with the situation. Society wants these boys put away so society is protected. The governor will tell you off the record that society is more at risk from these boys when they are released than when they went in. Anytime you know what is right and can't tell, for whatever reason, there must be corruption.[14]

This society has made cowards of us all. When the social services cannot do the things they were set up to do and they can't say so because of professional etiquette, that is corruption. Everybody has got to look as if they're doing their thing and coping properly.[15]

The disheartening thing is that the problem is so solvable. We could break the back of it in five years. But because of the hardening of stupid attitudes, and not even making the right approach.... The West Indian population in Britain is only half a million and that includes the children. Nearly two-thirds of this half million alone lives in London, the rest is between two or three large towns.[16] So you're not talking about any national gigantic programme of turning the educational system upside



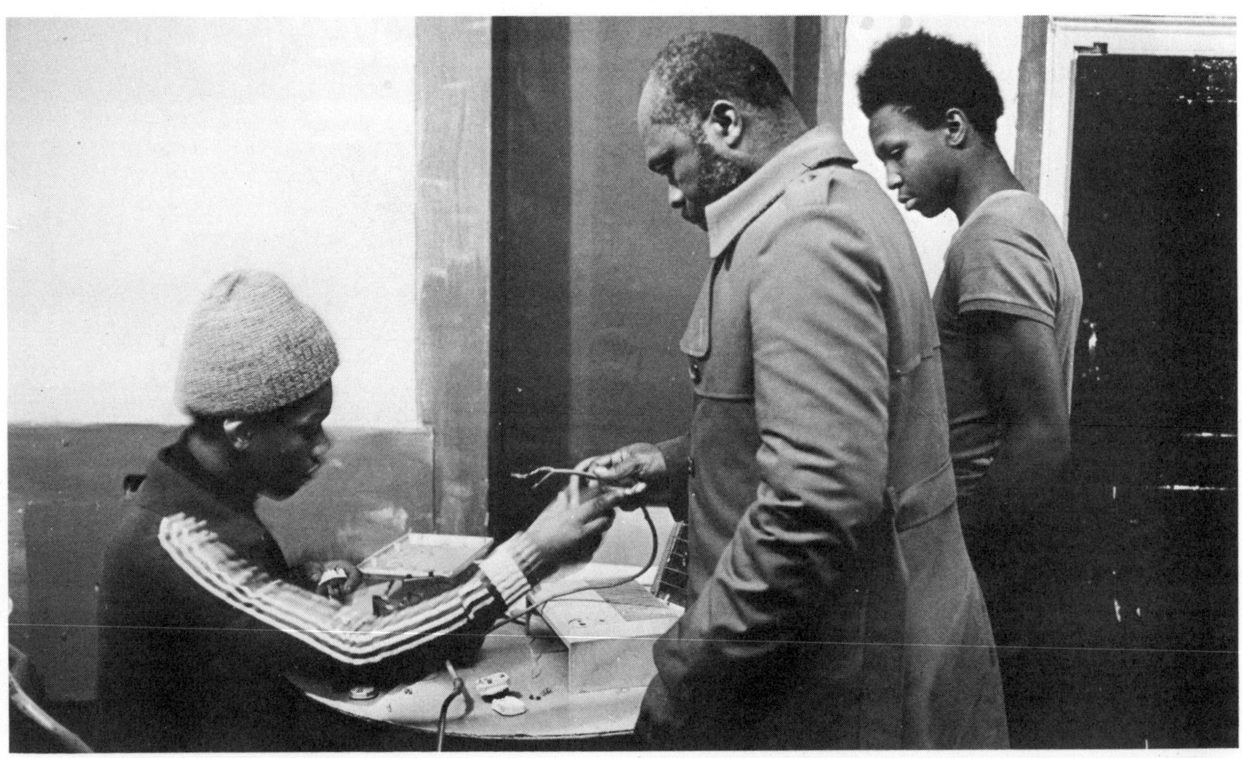

down.[17] A limited programme could break the back of the problem if only we could get the thinking and ethos right. It is crystal clear that we are having problems over and above other people, problems that are reflected out of all proportion to our number. These problems are fed on by West Indians as well, who haven't thought things out for themselves and who are simply in the old slavery thing of looking the white man in the eye and giving him the answers he wants to hear. They only want the esteem of white people.

We don't believe that anybody is obliged to help us. If we did we would get very angry and frustrated when they refused.

One is hoping that this course[18] will help. There will be six one-day seminars, films, discussions. At the end of six weeks people will go back to their work and work through their own situations. They'll be given opportunities to meet West Indians in their homes. They'll be establishing contact with tutors in a friendly social atmosphere. At the end of the two months we'll come together for a weekend and look at what benefits there have been.

We're going to take those who come in groups of three or four. If the course is going to achieve anything, it's a change in attitude. If we take just one bright spark from a department and put him or her back in the department where he doesn't have the support of others that have done the course, that is going to be putting him in the same position as we're in here – taking on every-body else. . . . "

17 School pupils with New Commonwealth backgrounds were only about 4 per cent of the total school population in the mid-1970s. More than half of these young people were in the London area, followed by south Lancashire and the West Midlands.

18 Westindian Concern Ltd ran a course in 1977 on 'The Westindian in Britain', inviting teachers, social workers, judges, etc., to learn more about West Indian family life and problems — as described by West Indians themselves. Do you think courses like this are a good way to try to influence the people who make decisions affecting West Indians?

● Has Ashton Gibson said anything that:
. . . surprised you?
. . . puzzled you?
. . . shocked you?
. . . worried you?
. . . angered you?

# Resources

**Books**
Ash, R. *Talking About Race* (Wayland 1974)
Curry, J. *Investigation into the Colour Problem* (Blackie 1974)
Hooper, F. *Language of Prejudice* (Penguin Connexions series 1969)
Hurman, A. *As Others See Us* (Edward Arnold 1977)
Last, M. *Race Relations in Britain* (Longman 1978)
Moss, P. *Prejudice and Discrimination* (Harrap Counterpoint series 1976)
Rogers, J. *Foreign Places, Foreign Faces* (Penguin Connexions series 1970)
SCM *Community Relations* (Probe Series 1973)

**Filmstrip**
*Understanding the Difference* (15 minutes, colour) Race Relations Employment
  Advisers (RREAS), free loan

**Films**
*Not Our Custom* (20 minutes) BBC Enterprises
*'Disgusted', Binchester* (9 minutes, colour cartoon) Central Film Library
*I'm Here* (15 minutes, colour) Concord
*The Family of Man* (50 minutes, colour) Concord
*Somebody's Daughter* (5 films, 20 minutes each) ILEA *You in the Seventies* series
*Asians on the Shop Floor* (25 minutes) RREAS, free loan
*I'll Just Ask Daddyji* (37 minutes, colour) The Other Cinema

More films on the subject of New Commonwealth immigrants can be obtained from
  Concord Films Council, 201 Felixstowe Road, Ipswich, Suffolk

**Addresses**
Centre for World Development Education (CWDE)
Parnell House, 25 Wilton Road, London SW1
Tel: 01–828 7611
A variety of low-cost information materials and visual aids on Asia, Africa and
Latin America (including countries of origin of New Commonwealth Immigrants)

Commission for Racial Equality (CRE)
Elliott House, 10–12 Allington Street, London SW1
Tel: 01–828 7022
A variety of free and low-cost information sheets, books, booklets and visual aids
related to immigrants in Britain and the countries from which they have come.

Commonwealth Institute
Kensington High Street, London W8
Tel: 01–602 3252
A variety of low-cost information materials and visual aids on all Commonwealth
countries, including the New Commonwealth.

*New Society* Readers' Service
2614 King's Reach Tower, Stamford Street, London SE1
Tel: 01–261 5239
A low-cost pamphlet guide to the 1976 Race Relations Act.

The following other organisations may also be able to provide information:

Action Group on Immigration and Nationality, 44 Theobalds Road, London WC1
Anti-Apartheid Movement, 89 Charlotte Street, London W1
British Council of Churches, Community and Race Relations Unit, 10 Eaton Grove,
  London SW1.
Institute of Race Relations, 247 Pentonville Road, London N1
Runnymede Trust, Stuart House, 1 Tudor Street, London EC4

© Nance Lui Fyson (words)
and Sally Greenhill (photos) 1979



First published 1979

Published by
MACMILLAN EDUCATION LIMITED
Houndmills Basingstoke Hampshire RG21 2XS
and London
Associated companies in Delhi Dublin
Hong Kong Johannesburg Lagos Melbourne
New York Singapore and Tokyo

Printed in Hong Kong

*British Library Cataloguing in Publication Data*

Fyson, Nance Lui
   Investigating society.
   Book 3: New Commonwealth immigrants.
   1. Great Britain – Social conditions – 1945 –
   I. Title.   II. Greenhill, Sally
   309.1'41'0857       HN385.5

   ISBN 0–333–25792–8
   ISBN 0–333–21684–9   Pbk